HERACLES

Heracles the Strong

Heracles

the Strong

By Ian Serraillier

Woodcuts by Rocco Negri

Henry Z. Walck, Inc.   *New York*

This Main Entry catalog card may be reproduced without permission.

Text copyright © 1970 by Ian Serraillier
Illustrations copyright © 1970 by Rocco Negri
All rights reserved
ISBN: 0-8098-2071-4
Library of Congress Catalog Card Number: 70-119574
Printed in the United States of America

Acknowledgments

The author is grateful for the valuable help and guidance he has received from the following books:

Euripides. *Alcestis and Other Plays,* translated by Philip Vellacott (Penguin Books, Inc.)
    Medea and Other Plays, translated by Philip Vellacott (Penguin Books, Inc.)
Graves, Robert. *The Greek Myths* (George Braziller, Inc.)
Kerenyi, C. *The Gods of the Greeks* (Vanguard Press, Inc.)
    The Heroes of the Greeks (Grove Press, Inc.)
Lempriere, J. *Classical Dictionary* (E. P. Dutton & Co., Inc.)
Loeb Classical Library. *Apollodorus, Apollonius Rhodius, Euripides, Ovid: The Metamorphoses, Sophocles, Theocritus* (Harvard University Press)
Sophocles. *Electra and Other Plays,* translated by E. F. Watling (Penguin Books, Inc.)
Warner, Rex. *Men and Gods* (Random House, Inc.)

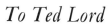

To Ted Lord

Contents

Heracles the Strong

1

The Monster Snakes

Heracles was the son of Zeus, the Father of the gods, but he was born into the mortal family of Amphitryon, the warrior Prince of Thebes. His mother was Alcmena, the wisest and most beautiful woman of her day. Her other son, whose father was Amphitryon, was called Iphicles. He was only a day younger than his brother. When they were barely ten months old, they had an adventure which brought them face to face with death and showed their different natures.

One evening, after Alcmena had bathed them and given them their milk, she put them to bed in the huge bronze shield which her husband had won in battle and which she proudly used as a cradle. Though she was a princess, she looked after the children herself. With her own hands she had made their saffron-dyed swaddling clothes and lamb-fleece coverlet.

"Sleep sweetly, my darlings," she said, as she tucked them in. "Wake happily in the morning."

Then she sang to them and rocked the shield until they were fast asleep.

At midnight, when the constellation of the Bear hung low in the western sky and all the household slept, two monster snakes came gliding over the threshold, over the marble floor toward the nursery. Their eyes were shooting flame; deadly poison dripped from their fangs. Hera, Queen of the gods, had sent them. Because Heracles was Alcmena's child and not her own, she was violently jealous of him and meant to kill him.

The nursery doors swung open without a sound. On and on glided the snakes. When they reached the bronze shield, they reared up, their blue coils bristling. They hovered above the babies with forked tongues flickering, ready to strike.

Suddenly the room was flooded with mysterious light. It seemed as if the marble pillars were lit from inside with luminous fire. It was Zeus who had done this, for there is nothing however secret that he does not see and know.

Iphicles screamed. He kicked off the coverlet and fell over the shield-rim to the floor.

Woken by the noise, Alcmena cried, "Get up, Amphitryon! The child is screaming. Something terrible must be happening."

Amphitryon sprang from the cedar bed. There was no time to put on his sandals or reach for his belt. From the wall peg he grabbed his brazen silver-studded sword and drew it from the sheath. At that moment the mysterious light drained away and the house was plunged in darkness.

"Where are my slaves?" he shouted. "Get up, and unbar the doors. Light your torches at the hearth. . . . Get up, I say. It is your master calling."

Drowsily the servants spilled from the hall benches where they were lying. They dipped their torches in the smoldering embers, then ran after their master and mistress into the nursery. In the smoky torchlight they saw Heracles sitting up in the cradle. The snakes were entwined about his body, tightening their scaly coils, trying to hug him to death.

Alcmena cried out in horror. The serving women started wailing and wringing their hands.

But Heracles had seized the snakes by the neck. His eyes were shining, as he held out the loathsome creatures for his father to see. Then, laughing and rejoicing in his strength, he squeezed with all his might. The jaws gaped open, the poison from the fangs dripped to the floor. At last the snakes lay slack and lifeless in his chubby hands, and he tossed them down in triumph at his father's feet.

None dared touch them. They shrank back in silence and stared at the forked tongues that flickered no more, at the blue luster of the scales growing dimmer as they watched, till they were dull as dust.

Iphicles lay on the floor whimpering, pale with fear. His

mother picked him up and took him to her room. Amphitryon picked up the other child and laid him in the cradle, tucking the coverlet around him. Then he went back to bed. The slaves put out the torches and lay down. Soon the household was asleep again.

But Alcmena could not sleep. She lay wide-eyed and still, while the sluggish hours dragged on to cockcrow. Then she got up and sent a servant to fetch old Teiresias, the blind prophet who used the song of birds to read the future. He hobbled into the hall, leaning on his stick.

"Sit down, good Teiresias," she said. She guided him to his ivory chair and told him what had happened. "What does it mean? Do the gods intend some disaster for us? I know that no one can escape his fate. You must tell me the truth."

Teiresias assured her that she had nothing to fear. "Noble lady, your people love you. The women of Argos, as they card the soft wool about their knees at evening, will sing your name and honor you always. As for your son Heracles, his days will shine with glory—I swear it, by the sweet light that left my eyes so long ago. He will be a hero without rival, master of the wild beasts and of all mankind. And when his mortal days come to an end, he will climb to the starry sky and live in the house of Zeus.

"But first there is something you must do—you must purify your house. Gather sticks of bramble, gorse and briar, and pear-tree twigs dried by the harsh wind. At midnight light a fire with them and burn the two snakes to ashes. In the morning tell one of your maids to throw the ashes into the river. Then cleanse the house with sulfur fumes and salted holy water. Last of all, you must sacrifice a young boar to Almighty Zeus."

The old man stood up, pushed back his ivory chair, and bowed. Then he hobbled away, snail-slow, weighed down by his years. And the tapping of his stick along the marble corridors grew softer and softer and died away.

Alcmena did exactly as he had told her.

2

A Fit of Madness

Heracles was brought up as Amphitryon's son, and his mother looked after him with the same watchful care that a gardener gives to a young sapling that he prizes. He was taught to read and sing and play the lyre, to study the wisdom of the past and the language of the stars. For a time he became the pupil of the Centaur Chiron, who lived in a cave on Mount Pelion and taught music, medicine and archery to the sons of princes and heroes. Heracles learned how to shoot, to stretch the string of ox's sinew to his chest and hoop the bow, then with a twang send the arrow straight to the mark. In time he was to excel all the archers of his day, even his friend Alcon, who could cleave a willow twig balanced on the point of a sword. Boxing became a favorite sport. With thongs of oxhide strapped to his fists, Heracles had a mighty punch and soon picked up the tricks—feinting, ducking, scaring his foe with frowns—and the tricks of the wrestler too, his falls and trips and rough-and-tumble cunning. He took instruction in warfare and learned how to protect himself against the cut and thrust of a sword, how at the crucial moment to swing his shield over his back and attack with his lance.

Amphitryon, himself a great charioteer who had won many trophies, taught him how to drive a chariot, to urge on the fiery horses and turn corners without grazing the marker stones. Always active, the youth wore a short tunic like a soldier's and spent his days in the open. His dinner was a plate of roast meat and a basketful of black bread; for supper he ate only plain uncooked food. Deeply attached to his father, he slept in a bed next to his, with a lion-skin for coverlet.

This was not the same lion-skin as he wore during the daytime. He came by this later, when he was eighteen and living with herdsmen on a cattle ranch near Thebes. A lion from the wooded slopes of Mount Cithaeron had begun to ravage his father's herds, and at once he set off to destroy it. On the way he plucked out a wild olive tree, bushy roots and all, then trimmed it into a club. After stalking the lion for many days, he at last tracked it down and killed it with the club. Then he stripped the pelt and ever afterward wore it as a cloak, with his head framed in the gaping jaws.

His next success was the defeat of the Minyans, when

they marched against Thebes to exact an unjust tribute. He ambushed them in a narrow pass and destroyed them almost single-handed. As a reward Creon, the grateful King of Thebes, convinced that Heracles was the bravest and strongest man on earth, gave him his daughter Princess Megara for wife. To the joyous music of flutes, the young hero brought her home to Amphitryon's palace.

He was devoted to her and to their three sons. When he was away on his journeys, as he often was, the boys kept asking, "Mother, where has he gone? When will he be back?" If they heard the gate open, they ran to see if it was he, then clambered over him and smothered him with kisses. The marriage brought him great happiness. But it also brought him suffering and tragedy and appalling trials.

One day, just back from an adventure, after the joyous reunion with his family he went to the altar to offer sacrifice for his safe return. Suddenly the goddess Hera, in her spite and jealousy, drove him blindly mad. Like a whirlwind he raged through the palace. Without knowing what he was doing, he killed two of his sons. Megara snatched the youngest one away and ran with him to her room and locked the door. But Heracles smashed the doorposts and with a single blow killed them both. Then, as suddenly as it had come, the madness passed, and he dropped senseless to the ground. Quickly Amphitryon and the servants tied him fast with ropes to a pillar.

After a while he woke. He was stupefied and bewildered.

"What are these ropes doing?" he shouted. "Why have

you fastened me with moorings like a ship? These broken benches—my arrows scattered everywhere—what do they mean? Will nobody explain?"

He saw Amphitryon trembling by the door.

"Father, why are you afraid to come near me? Why are you in tears?"

"Your life is in ruins," said Amphitryon. "Your sufferings would make even the gods weep."

"I do not understand. Speak plainly." And when no one would answer, he shouted, "Undo these ropes and I will find out for myself."

Nervously Amphitryon untied the ropes, and Heracles stood up. When he saw the bodies, he was at first too stunned and horrified to speak. Then, reaching for his bow, he cried, "Who killed them?"

"You did," said Amphitryon. "But you were out of your mind. It was not your fault."

"And my wife? Did I kill her too?"

"You killed them all."

In grief and shame he sank to his knees beside Megara and buried his face in her gown.

"I can remember nothing. Where was I when this madness attacked me?"

"By the altar. You were washing your hands for the sacrifice. . . . But I tell you, it was not your fault. The goddess Hera sent the madness."

"That is no excuse," said Heracles. "I murdered them. The crime was mine, and I must pay for it with my life."

He got up and ran outside, ready to throw himself from a cliff-top or plunge a sword in his heart. No one, not even Amphitryon, dared stand in his way.

On the palace steps he stopped. The courtyard was full, and a man was marching forward to greet him. It was Theseus, King of Athens, his closest friend, attended by his courtiers.

Covering his head with his cloak, Heracles turned back into the palace and knelt again by the bodies.

Puzzled by his reception, Theseus followed him in. When he saw the chaos in the room, he thought at first that some enemy must have invaded Thebes to seize the throne. Then Amphitryon explained what had happened, and how Hera's cruel hand was responsible for the slaughter.

"But why does your son cover his head and refuse to greet me?"

"Through shame and grief."

"But I am here to share his grief," said Theseus. "Uncover his head."

But when his father tried to do so, Heracles waved him angrily away and shouted to Theseus to stand back. "I am a murderer, and if you touch me you will be defiled."

"I am not afraid of defilement," said Theseus. "True friendship cannot be tainted."

"Do you realize what I have done?"

"I can see for myself." Gently he lifted the cloak from his friend's head. "Stand up, Heracles, and look me in the face. A brave spirit can bear the blows of fate without flinching—all the more so when he has a friend who will share his suffering. Your sorrows cry out to heaven, and you need my help and sympathy." He held out his arms and clasped the bloodstained hands.

"What else can I do but kill myself?" said Heracles. "I have destroyed my family. I shall be rejected wherever I go. What hope have I against Hera's cruel cunning? When I was still in the cradle, she sent two monster snakes to strangle me—and now this violent madness. She will not rest till she has destroyed me."

"I understand how you feel," said Theseus. "But you must not kill yourself, for suffering comes to every man. You must be strong and endure. Come back with me to Athens. I will give you a house and money and all the gifts my grateful people gave me when I slew the evil Minotaur. We shall be proud to welcome you. Your presence will honor us."

For a long time Heracles was silent, swallowed in despair. To Theseus he was not guilty of murder, as he had not known what he was doing. But Heracles could not think the matter out at all. Gradually, he came to see that it would be cowardly to kill himself. He must face the world and endure the blows of fortune, like any other man.

At last he said, "Very well, Theseus. I will be strong and patient. For your gifts and kindness I thank you with all my heart. I will gladly go with you to Athens."

Sadly he said good-bye to his dead loved ones. He asked his father to bury them in one grave and lay the children in their mother's arms, close to her heart.

Then he looked at the bow which he had used to kill them. In all his battles it had served him well, yet how he loathed it now! "It reminds me of my guilt, it torments me. But I must learn to live with it. I shall take it with me."

He slung it over his shoulder and, without a backward glance, followed Theseus out of the palace.

3

The Nemean Lion

Heracles did not stay long at Athens. His heart was numb with misery, and he could not shake off his feelings of guilt.

"I must go to Delphi to consult the oracle and be purified," he told Theseus. "But I shall never forget your kindness. If ever you needed me, I would cross the world to help you."

So he went to Delphi, where the sunlight flashes from the cliffs and all day long the eagles circle overhead. In the Temple of Apollo the priestess, after bathing in the holy spring, received him. Dressed in the robes of prophecy, she led him to the inmost shrine, where she sat down on Apollo's three-legged throne. Then Heracles knelt and asked her how he could be purified of his sin.

Before answering, she filled the bowl of the tripod in front of her with laurel leaves and set light to them. Then, breathing in the fumes, she gazed at the golden image of the god gleaming in the darkness and fell into a trance. Soon she was crying out wild and frenzied words. But as the wishes of the god became clear, her voice steadied and she told Heracles his penance. "You must go to Mycenae to your cousin King Eurystheus and serve him for twelve years. If you do faithfully whatever he commands, you will be made immortal and live forever with the gods."

"Twelve years of slavery?" The harsh sentence filled Heracles with despair. He knew Eurystheus was a coward. He could not bear the thought of serving a lesser man than himself. Then he cursed himself for giving way to his feelings. Pulling himself together, "Priestess," he said, "the punishment is just. I will go willingly."

He marched through the valley of gray-blue olive trees, down to the rippling waters of the Gulf of Corinth. Here he took a boat to the desolate shore on the other side. He climbed the mountain and passed between the raw lonely summits, through the craggy defiles, down the steep scrubby slopes. The great plain of Argos stretched out before him. Half-hidden in the purple shadows was the fortress palace of Mycenae, and far beyond it the blue waters of the Bay of Nauplia. He could see no farms or homesteads, only shaggy goats foraging among the rocks, and lower down fields of corn and barley springing from the rich red earth. At last, following a dusty track through a grove of eucalyptus trees, he came upon the massive crouching walls of the palace fortress. So huge were the roughhewn stones that it seemed that only giants could have put them there.

As if expecting him, the gates swung open on their bronze pivots. He marched in past the guards into the King's room. It was small and square, with a round hearth from which four blood-red wooden pillars rose to support the roof. Beyond them, framed between, sat Eurystheus on his ebony throne, a timid guardian for that bleak forbidding place. And before him stood the strongest man on earth.

"The oracle has sent me here to serve you," said Heracles. "Tell me, sir, what I must do."

Eurystheus glared at him, his eyes full of hatred. Here was a chance to humiliate a man who had all the strength and valor that he himself so obviously lacked. When he answered Heracles, his words were crisp and harsh. He was like a dog that barks furiously, but at the stir of a step slinks away with its tail between its legs.

"In the forests of Nemea there is a savage lion. It ravages our northern land like a flood, and no one can kill it, for no iron, bronze or stone can pierce its skin. Destroy it and bring me the skin as proof that it is dead."

This was the first of twelve labors that Eurystheus imposed on him.

Before he left for Nemea, the gods loaded him with gifts of armor. Apollo gave him a bow and arrows trimmed with eagle feathers; Hephaestos the fire-god, a golden breastplate, bronze greaves and helmet; and Zeus, an unbreakable shield

with stories worked on the face in enamel and lapis lazuli. Carved around the boss were twelve serpents' heads. When the hero marched into battle, they clashed their jaws, striking terror in the heart of the enemy.

But Heracles despised armor and set off for Nemea without them. All he took were his bow and arrows and his hunter's club.

Soon he came to some waste country, where all the crops had been trampled down and the boundary walls wrecked. On a lonely mountainside beyond was a shepherd's cottage, and here he asked to stay the night. The lion had already killed the shepherd's son. When he was told of his guest's brave errand, the shepherd wanted to sacrifice a ram in his honor.

"Wait till I come back," said Heracles. "Then you can sacrifice it to Zeus for protecting me. If after thirty days I have not returned, then you can sacrifice it in memory of me."

All next day Heracles searched, but it was not till evening that he spotted the lion's trail. It led to a cave, whose double mouth was strewn with bones. He just had time to hide in the undergrowth outside, when the lion came bounding out of the wood. The day's slaughter had splashed the lion's beard with blood, which it licked with relish.

Heracles shot an arrow at its left flank, but it bounced off, without even grazing the flesh. The lion raised its tawny head, looked around in amazement, then roared.

Heracles shot another arrow, this time at its heart. But it did no more damage than a pebble flung at a wall. Contemptuously the lion lashed its tail, then turned and disappeared into the cave. To prevent escape, Heracles blocked up one of the entrances with boulders, then plunged inside into the darkness.

Soon he heard the sound of snores, booming and echoing in the hollow cavern. The lion was asleep, gorged with prey. As he came near, the stench of breath steaming from its mouth and nostrils was suffocating. He raised his club to strike—then tripped. The lion woke, its angry eyes burning up the darkness. As soon as it saw the intruder, curving its spine like a bow it crouched, ready to spring.

But Heracles was too quick. He broke his club over its head. Half-stunned, the beast wagged its head drunkenly; the flames in its eyes flickered and grew dim. He sprang at its throat, pressed his thumbs deep into the iron flesh and choked it to death. Then he dragged the carcass to the entrance.

He looked down at the armored hide. Neither stone nor steel nor anything else could pierce it—how could he strip it then for Eurystheus? Suddenly he had an idea. The lion's claws were razor-sharp—why not use them? So he cut them off, flayed the carcass with them, and draped the skin over his shoulders like a cloak. Then he returned to Mycenae, not forgetting to stop at the shepherd's cottage to join in the sacrifice. And he also cut himself a new club.

His arrival at the palace created some alarm. Eurystheus was standing on a platform directing a repair to the walls, when he saw what he took to be the Nemean lion coming at him. He was so terrified that he fell off, and with a howl of pain he limped away and hid. When a servant came to tell him that it was only Heracles and that he had brought back the lion's hide, he refused to see him.

"Tell Heracles he is never to enter the city again," he said. "In the future he can wait outside the gates for his orders."

Then he told his bronzesmith to forge him a brazen jar big enough to hide in, and he had it sunk into the earth. Safe inside, he cautiously lifted the lid and shouted for a herald.

"Go to Heracles and inform him of his second task," he said. "He is to go at once to the green marshes of Argos. There, in the bottomless waters of Lerna, the Hydra, the murderous water snake, has made its lair. His orders are to kill it."

And he closed the lid with a bang.

4

The Nine-Headed Hydra

So Heracles set off to kill the Hydra. This time he did not go alone; his nephew Iolaus, the son of Iphicles, went with him as his charioteer, the reins flowing from his fingers as the horses galloped.

In the narrow strip of land between the hills of Lerna and the gulf, there is a sacred cavern. Below it a river gushes from the rock, then widens into marshy streams on its way to the sea. The grass here is green and fresh, and gigantic plane trees with twisted roots reach upward to the sky. But the marsh is pestilent, a breeding place for flies. It was the haunt of the Hydra, the nine-headed water snake that ravaged the herds and filled the countryside with terror.

When the chariot wheels were bogged down in the marsh, Heracles jumped out and squelched through the shallows, searching for the monster. Soon, to see what all the splashing was about, the Hydra lifted its nine heads one by one above the water. Heracles let fly with his arrows. Angrily thrashing the swamp, the Hydra raced toward him and twined its slippery coils about his feet, trying to overthrow him. Heracles stood firm. Swinging his club, he battered each head in turn.

But as soon as one head was crushed, two more sprang up in its place. The forked tongues spat out breath so venomous that the hero was weakening fast. When a huge crab scuttled out from between the tree roots and tried to claw him down into the swamp, it seemed that all was lost. He clubbed its shell, and shouted to Iolaus for help.

"Cut down some branches from the plane trees," he cried. "Set them alight and burn out the roots of all these sprouting heads."

It was the only way he could think of to stop the heads from increasing, and Iolaus obeyed with lightning speed. Soon only one head was left. It was immortal, and part of it was made of gold. Since he could not destroy it, Heracles cut it off with his sword and buried it under a rock, the forked tongue still hissing.

All around him, flattening the reeds and grass, lay the

monster's lifeless coils, with poison oozing from them. Before returning to Mycenae, Heracles dipped his arrows in the poison. Ever afterward the least scratch from them was fatal.

Eurystheus was not at all impressed with this success. He blamed Heracles for accepting his nephew's help and at once sent him off on another labor. This time he was to go to the desolate woods and mountains of Arcadia to hunt down and bring home alive a dappled hind that was causing great destruction in the peasants' fields. This hind was swifter than the wind, had brazen hooves and golden branching antlers, and was sacred to Artemis, the archer-goddess of hunting. But the strangest thing about it was that it cast such a spell on its pursuer that he could not stop chasing it.

For a whole year, Heracles hunted it all over the world. But at last, back in Arcadia once more, he saw the hind running down the mountainside to the river, where it collapsed, exhausted. Careful not to hurt it, Heracles shot and pinned its forelegs with an arrow that passed between bone and sinew without drawing blood. Then he picked it up, laid it across his shoulders, and started back for Mycenae.

On the way, as Heracles was passing through a wood, an archer sprang out from the trees and stopped him. It was the archer-goddess Artemis. She was more like a boy than a woman.

"That hind is sacred to me," she cried, with flashing eyes. "Why have you captured it?"

"You must blame Eurystheus, who forced me to do it.

I have been careful not to hurt the beast," he answered.

"See you look after it," said Artemis, her eyes softening. "When you have shown it to Eurystheus, let it go. It belongs to the woods and mountains."

When he returned to Mycenae, he did not forget the goddess's command.

His next task was to go to the cypress-covered slopes of Mount Erymanthus and bring back the wild boar that was raging there. He had to pass through the land of the Centaurs, rugged creatures who were men only to the waist and below that had the body and legs of a horse. One of them, whose name was Pholus, entertained him in his cave and gave him a plate of roast meat. When Heracles asked for a drink, Pholus opened a special jar of wine that had been given to all the Centaurs and not to him alone. Attracted by the smell, the rest came galloping in. When they saw what he had done, they were furious. With rocks and axes and uprooted fir trees they swarmed around Heracles and attacked him. While Pholus hid in terror, Heracles pelted them with brands he had pulled from the fire and drove them out of the cave. Then he let fly at them with his poisoned arrows, scattering them all over the plain.

Some escaped to the cave of Chiron, the wise and gentle Centaur who had for a time been schoolmaster to Heracles. Unfortunately one arrow went straight through a Centaur's arm into Chiron's knee and stuck there, quivering. In great distress Heracles ran to his old friend and drew out the shaft.

He gave him medicine and tried to dress the wound, but all in vain—the Hydra's poison was too strong. Howling with pain, Chiron limped into his cave, crying out, "Father Zeus, hear my prayer. I am the only Centaur that you made immortal. But the pain of my wound is more than I can bear— O, let me die."

Zeus granted him his wish at once, and the gentle Centaur breathed his last. But Heracles could not forgive himself for what he had done. While he buried his old friend, his shoulders shook with weeping.

The other dead Centaurs were buried by Pholus, who did not however survive them long. Puzzled to find that some of them were hardly marked and that tiny scratches could be so deadly, he picked up an arrow to examine it. It slipped from his fingers, pricked his foot and killed him.

Sadly Heracles continued his search for the wild boar. It was winter when he came across it hiding in a thicket by the river Erymanthus. With loud halloos he frightened it out, then chased it up the mountain to the highest passes, where the air was icy cold and the snow lay thick. In the deep drifts its short legs tired quickly. When it sank down exhausted, he sprang on its back and tied it up. Then he hoisted it over his shoulders and, wading through the snow, carried it down the mountain and back to Mycenae.

As he held it up for Eurystheus to see, the King took a flying leap into his bronze jar. This was a scene that the old Greek vase-painters loved to represent. One of them shows the hero leaning over the rim of the jar, with the wild boar slung over his shoulder. Snout and tusks point downward, the eyes are glaring. Above the rim of the buried jar, the King's head and outstretched fingers of one arm are visible, as he cries out, gibbering with terror.

5

The Stables of Augeias

The fifth labor of Heracles was to clean out the stables of King Augeias in a single day. They were filthy and had not been touched for years. As he gave the order, Eurystheus chuckled to think of Heracles, waist-deep in muck, heaping the dung into baskets and carrying it away.

Augeias, who had more flocks and herds of cattle than anyone in the world, lived on the western coast in the realm of the setting sun. It was a land of extraordinary beauty, with groves of wild olives and luxuriant plane trees, their leaves luminous in the dancing heat of summer.

As Heracles approached, it was early evening, and Helios the sun-god was driving his fiery chariot-horses toward the western rim of the sky. Shading his eyes, Heracles watched the sheep moving slowly from the pastures to their folds. Behind them came the cattle in the thousands, like a massive cloud rolled on by the south wind. The whole plain was bursting with them; the hills on either side echoed to their lowing. Heracles followed, enchanted. But as they neared the stables, the honey-sweet air gave way to a foul and pestilent stench. The crops in the fields were dry and withered; nothing, not even a weed, would grow.

Then Heracles caught sight of Augeias. He knew him by the sunbeams that streamed from his eyes, for Helios the sun-god was his father. Though Heracles was almost choking, Augeias was so used to the stench that he did not notice it. He was marching around his stalls, shouting to his herdsmen to treat the oxen with care, especially the two hundred red stud-bulls and the three hundred black bulls with crumpled horns. But his prize possession was twelve swan-white bulls that were sacred to his father Helios. He looked after these himself.

Suddenly one of them saw Heracles. From the tawny skin and the grim jaws that framed his head, it mistook him for a lion. Angrily pawing the ground and determined to kill him, with a fearful bellow the bull charged.

But Heracles stood his ground. He clutched the bull's left horn and leaned heavily on its neck, then pressed his shoulder against its flank and held it down.

The King and his son Phyleus were much impressed by the hero's rippling muscles and colossal strength. But they were also afraid that he might do the animal some lasting

harm, and were relieved when he loosened his grip and let it go.

"You do not need to tell me your name," said Augeias, when he had welcomed him. "I have heard all about you—and how you slew the lion that ravaged your father's herds. I like the use to which you have put its skin."

"The bull does not share your opinion," laughed Heracles.

"What brings you so far from home?"

"I have come to clean your stables," said Heracles. "What's more, sir, I will do it in a single day."

"Did you hear that, Phyleus?" said Augeias. "In a single day! Is he mad?"

"Make him swear to keep his word," said Phyleus.

"I will do so gladly," said Heracles. "But your father must swear to give me a tenth of his herds if I succeed."

"An excellent bargain," said Augeias, convinced the task was impossible.

And with Phyleus as witness they both swore their oaths.

In the morning Heracles made holes in the foundation walls of the stables. He dug a channel and changed the course of the river Alpheus. It came foaming and gushing through the gaps and washed all the filth into the sea. When the herds returned at evening, he had turned back the river to its usual bed and repaired the walls. For the first time in years the stone floors smelled fresh and clean.

Heracles went to Augeias and asked for his reward.

"My herald tells me you were under the orders of

Eurystheus," said the King. "You shall have nothing."

"But you swore an oath—your son was witness."

"I made no promises. I will give you nothing," stormed the King.

"Then my case must be heard in a court of law."

Even a man as mean as Augeias could hardly refuse that. A court was summoned and each party put its case. When the judges called on Phyleus, he testified that Heracles had spoken the truth and that his father had indeed promised him a tenth of all his herds.

"Then the King must keep his promise. He cannot break his word," the judges ruled.

Augeias lost his temper. "This lion-headed lout has tricked me!" he cried. "It was the river-god that did the work, not he! I banish him from my land forever. My son has disgraced me—I banish him as well."

Heracles would have knocked Augeias down; but he remembered he had come to expiate a crime and held himself in check.

"If that is how a king keeps his word," he scoffed, "how his people must despise him!" And he turned on his heel and went.

But there was little comfort for him at Mycenae. Eurystheus claimed that, as Heracles had worked for hire, the cleaning of the stables counted for nothing. And he soon devised another labor for him.

6

The Brass Rattle

In the northeastern corner of Arcadia, surrounded by pine-woods and mountains, lie the dark swampy waters of the Stymphalian Lake. A colony of birds lived here, among the rocks and along the reedy shore. They had come here to escape from wolves and were as big as swans and cranes, but much fiercer. Reared by Ares the war-god, they fed on human flesh. Their beaks and claws and wings were of bronze, and they attacked people by shooting their feathers at them like darts. But they were easily frightened. When disturbed, they flew up into the trees around the lake. The branches sagged under their weight as they sat there squawking, so thickly clustered that not a twig or pine needle could be seen. It looked as if the whole forest had sprouted leaves of bronze, which glowed in the sunlight like fire.

"These murderous birds are numberless as the waves of the sea," said Eurystheus. "If they are allowed to go on breeding, there will soon be no men left on earth." And he ordered Heracles to go at once and destroy them.

As soon as Heracles appeared by the lake, the startled birds flew up into the trees or hid among the rocks. He tried wading after them, but his legs sank deep into the mud and he could hardly move. He used the trunk of a fallen pine to make a boat and dragged it into the water, but the lake was too shallow for it.

Suddenly while he was standing on the shore wondering what to do next, the goddess Athene appeared in the eerie silence.

"I have brought you a gift," she said.

Gratefully he held out his hand, expecting it to be some weapon. But it was a huge brass rattle, and before he could ask her what use it was for killing birds she vanished.

There was only one thing to do with a rattle—shake it. So he shook it, leaping from rock to rock as he did so. The din, multiplied and echoed by the mountains, was ear-splitting. From their hiding places the birds streamed in terror into the air, darkening the sun like a thundercloud. The sky was as black as the Lake. As the darts began showering down, Heracles groped his way to the shelter of a cave, whirling his rattle all the time. With the clash of cymbals the panic-stricken birds collided in midair. Their wings hopelessly entangled, they fell into the Lake and drowned. But some escaped to the Isle of Ares in the Black Sea, where later they

were to attack the Argonauts on their voyage in search of the Golden Fleece. As the numbers in the sky lessened, the darkness turned to dusk and the dusk to daylight. Only a few stragglers were left, and Heracles brought them down easily with his arrows.

After the last of them had crashed to the rock at his feet, a great silence descended and the Lake was still, its surface uneven with broken wings like frozen waves of gold. The birds were all dead. Ever since then the lake has been a gentle place, the haunt of ducks and cranes and herons, of moorhens and waterfowl harmless to men.

Heracles picked up a handful of dead birds and, to prove that he had fulfilled his task, took them back to Mycenae. But Eurystheus made light of it. He pretended it was a joke for so great a hero to waste his time killing birds.

"I have another task for you, more worthy of your powers," he said. "Go to Crete, the island of Minos the sea-king, and bring back the bull that the sea-god Poseidon gave him. It has gone mad."

So Heracles took ship for Crete, where King Minos welcomed him in his palace at Cnossus. Set among fir trees along the crest of a hill, it had just been rebuilt after an earthquake and was more like a city than a palace. King Minos spent two whole days showing him around. He made him go up and down the grand new staircase several times, pointing proudly to the wells of light which lit each story. He took him through the halls and galleries and showed him the frescoes and wall paintings—of flower gardens, of a Prince of the Lilies—which the artists were still working on. Heracles liked best the pictures of young men of the court somersaulting over the horns of wild bulls, for they seemed to him full of the joy of life.

"But I did not come to look at pictures," he said impatiently. "What about that bull I was sent here to catch?"

King Minos seemed embarrassed by the question. "I promised to sacrifice to Poseidon whatever he sent me from the sea. But what should rise out of the waves but this magnificent creature, so sleek and beautiful, with scarlet ribbons tied to its horns? I could not bear to sacrifice it. So I let it go and sacrificed another instead. The god was furious. He made the bull go mad. And now it is ravaging the whole island, rooting up crops, knocking down walls. And I am entirely to blame. I should not have been so greedy and stupid. . . . But look at this picture my royal cupbearer finished yesterday—the paint is still wet. What do you think of it?"

"That we had better leave the paint to dry," said Heracles. And he wondered where King Minos had got his reputation for being a fearless warlord. There seemed to be nothing in his head but art. "Now where is the bull? And what help can you give me?"

"No help at all. Nobody here can do anything with it. We put all our confidence in you."

Heracles set out at once to find the bull. After pursuing it all over the island, at last he cornered it by some rocks on a riverbank. An ancient vase-painting shows how he threw a rope around its muzzle and foreleg; and when it started to breathe out scorching fire, he stunned it with his club.

King Minos was delighted. He wanted to reward Heracles with some of the treasures from his palace—a set of crystal goblets, a gold signet ring engraved with his portrait, a bronze helmet, a dagger inlaid with ivory. But Heracles refused them all. He returned at once with the bull to Mycenae, where he let it go. Snorting flame, it chased Eurystheus to his jar—he dived in, head first. Then it galloped off through the fields and over the mountains.

For a time it wandered about the Peloponnese. At last it crossed the isthmus and came to the Plain of Marathon, where it killed everyone who came near it, until Theseus caught it and sacrificed it to Athene.

7

The Fight With Death

The hero's next labor was to go to Thrace, the land of the north wind, and capture the four winged chariot-horses of King Diomede. The cruel King kept them chained to bronze mangers and fed them with the flesh of visitors. Heracles stunned him with his club, then threw him to the mares to eat. Once their hunger was satisfied, he tamed them easily and brought them back to Mycenae.

It was on his way to Thrace to perform this labor that he had an adventure which shows, most movingly, his noble and generous nature.

Having to pass through Thessaly, Heracles decided to spend a night at the house of his wealthy and hospitable friend, King Admetus. Although he did not know it, on the very day that he arrived the King's lovely young wife Alcestis had died, and in the strangest manner. By rights it was her husband who should have died, for the Fates had spun the thread of his life to the very end. At the last moment the Fates had been tricked into letting him escape; but they had made one condition—that he should find someone else to take his place. This had not been an easy task, for most people like to cling onto life as long as they can. He had asked his old father, pointing out that he could not in any case expect to live much longer or get much enjoyment from life, but the only answer he had received was an angry refusal. He had asked his mother, all his family in turn, with no better success. Only one person had been willing to die for him, his young and beautiful wife Alcestis.

"I will take your place because I honor and respect you," she told him. "I hope the gods will protect my children and not let them die before their time, like their mother." The two children, a boy and a girl, burst into tears and clung to her dress. She picked them up and kissed them and said good-bye.

The servants too were broken-hearted. Admetus, feeling very sorry for himself, embraced his wife sadly and begged her not to leave him.

"The gods may still be merciful and spare you," he said. "If not, I shall spend the rest of my life mourning you."

By the time Heracles arrived, Death had already come for Alcestis and taken her, and the palace was full of grief and lamentation. In spite of his despair, Admetus felt that he could not turn an honored guest away. Even at a time like this, a host should not neglect his duties. He must be welcoming and hide his own grief. So he invited the traveler in.

"Why is your hair cut short?" said Heracles. "Are you in mourning for someone?"

"I have a funeral to attend."

"Not one of your children, I hope?"

"No, they are both well."

"Your father or your mother, or—"

"A close friend of the family," said Admetus quickly. "She lived in the house with us."

"I am deeply sorry," said Heracles. "I would not have come, had I known. I will leave at once."

But Admetus would not hear of his going. It was not his habit to turn guests away. Besides, whenever he went to Argos, Heracles had made him heartily welcome. He told the servants to take his guest to another room, where he could eat and enjoy himself on his own, away from sounds of mourning.

So Admetus went sadly to the funeral, and Heracles dined alone. He was very hungry and, as he was not interfering with anyone else, he saw no reason why he should not enjoy himself. He put garlands on his head; he ate with relish the pile of meat in front of him; he downed cup after cup of wine and kept shouting for more. Soon he was roaring drunk, and singing at the top of his voice.

The servants were disgusted. They could not help comparing his manners with those of their mistress, who had always been so gentle, so considerate to them. And what a sympathetic wife she had been, understanding their master's moods, calming him down whenever he was in a rage. But Admetus had given them strict orders to keep quiet about her death. They turned their heads away, careful not to let Heracles see the tears in their eyes.

"Why are you all so solemn?" he cried. "We've all got to die sometime or other. Stop scowling there in the corner. Come over here and join me in a cup of wine."

But they shrank away.

"We are not in the mood for drinking," said one of the cupbearers.

"You take it too much to heart. Why, the dead woman was not even a close member of the family. She was only a friend."

"Only a friend?"

"That is what Admetus said. Or are you trying to tell me that he lied?"

Heracles tottered over to the cupbearer and fixed him with a glance of fire. "You are hiding something from me," he shouted. "Who is it that has died?"

"His wife Alcestis," said the cowering servant.

Heracles threw down his cup. He stumbled back to his couch and buried his head in his hands. "I ought to have guessed it," he said, bitterly remorseful. "Admetus was in mourning. There were tears in his eyes. He said he was weeping for a stranger, and I believed him. What a blundering idiot I've been! To get drunk in this tragic house—O, why did you let me do it?"

"Our master forbade us to tell you the truth. He wanted you to be happy, even though he was in despair."

"Then I shall return his kindness with kindness. Where is he burying her? Where can I find the tomb?"

"On the outskirts of the city, on the road to Larissa. You will find it there."

Out of the palace ran Heracles to find the tomb. The mourners would now be there sacrificing, and, when they left, Death himself would come to drink the blood-offerings. I will hide behind the tomb and spring out on him, he thought. I will grapple him in my arms and squeeze the breath out of his body till he gives Alcestis up. But if he does not come, I must go down to the sunless kingdom of the dead and fetch her back. I will not rest until I have given her safe into Admetus's hands.

Buoyed up at the thought of another wrestling match, he ran all the way to the tomb.

After the funeral the mourners went sadly home. Back in the palace again without his beloved wife, Admetus was overwhelmed with loneliness. Everything he looked at—her chair, her bed, the weeping children—reminded him of her. What pleasure could there be in going on living now? He began to feel that he had been wrong to let her die for him. His enemies would talk behind his back and despise him for being a coward.

All day long he sat on the palace steps, weighed down

with grief and guilt. In the evening he saw two figures come into the courtyard. One of them was Heracles. There were beads of sweat on his skin and he looked utterly exhausted. The other figure, whom he led by the hand, was a woman, heavily veiled.

"Admetus, you should have told me the truth," said Heracles. "You should not have let me drink and make merry in a house of mourning."

"I could not turn you away, and I did not want to make you miserable. I had sorrows enough of my own."

"And I will not add to them now," said Heracles. "I am going to Thrace to fetch the wild horses of King Diomede, and I'd like to ask you a favor before I leave. Will you take this woman into your house and keep her until I come back? I won her today in a wrestling match."

"What, after the loss I have just suffered? How could I take her?"

"Look carefully at her, Admetus."

Although Admetus could not see her face, there was something about the way she stood that reminded him of his wife and made his eyes fill with tears. "She looks too much like Alcestis. Why do you torment me, Heracles? O, take her away! No woman in the world could take the place of my dead wife."

"I know how much you loved her. But be generous, invite this woman in. Take her hand in yours."

"You cannot compel me."

With a laugh Heracles seized their two hands and joined

them together. "You have her now. Keep her forever," he said, and lifted the veil from her head.

"Great son of Zeus! My wife—alive! Can I touch her? Can I speak to her? How did you get her from the kingdom of darkness?"

"I fought with Death behind her tomb and made him give her back."

"Why does she not speak to me?"

"She still belongs to the gods below. It will be three days before you can hear her voice. Take her into the house, for I have work to do and must go. Good-bye, Admetus."

And away he went to Thrace to perform his labor.

8

The Three-Bodied Giant

After bringing back King Diomede's horses, Heracles was sent to fetch the gold-embroidered belt of Hippolyta, Queen of the riding Amazons. They were a tribe of warrior women who lived by a river mouth on the shores of the Black Sea and spent their lives fighting. Hippolyta was the tallest and bravest of them all. Spear in hand, dressed in a skirt and long Scythian trousers, the helmeted Queen received him courteously and was quite willing to let him have the belt as a present. But the goddess Hera, disguised as an Amazon, had spread about a mischievous rumor that Heracles had come to kidnap her. Angrily the warrior women seized their brazen bows and half-moon shields, mounted their horses and swept down on the stranger's ship. Afraid of treachery, Heracles killed Hippolyta and took her belt and spear. After scattering the rest, he sailed back home.

His tenth labor took him farther west than he had ever been before, to the Island of the Sunset Glow, near the stream of Ocean, where Geryon lived. Geryon was a giant with three bodies growing out of his waist. Said to be the strongest man alive, he owned a herd of purple-red cattle, guarded by a herdsman and a two-headed watchdog named Orthos. Heracles was told to kill him, seize the cattle and drive them the long way back to Argos. On his way there, at the entrance of the Mediterranean where Spain looks across the narrow straits to Africa, he set up two brass pillars, one on either side. These came to be known among sailors as the Pillars of Heracles. Some say that he put them there to make the straits narrow and discourage whales and other sea monsters from entering. Others claim that before his arrival Europe and Africa were joined together, and that he cut a channel between the two.

It was not an easy journey. As he trudged across the deserts of North Africa, knee-deep in burning sand, he looked up at the sun-god in the sky and cried out, "All-seeing, all-hearing Father Sun, with your chariot and your horses swifter than the wind, have pity on me! You are scorching me to death."

He lost his temper and shot an arrow at the handsome young god. It glanced past the cheek-piece of his helmet and sped harmlessly on.

The sun-god looked down at him. Brilliant rays streamed

from his eyes; his thick cloak flashed like lightning. "Put down your bow," he said.

Heracles obeyed. His anger had vanished, and he apologized.

"You must think before you act," said the sun-god. "But I admire your strength and the courage you bring to your task. I would not like you to fail." And he lent him a great gold cup shaped like a water-lily, in which the hero sailed from the African coast all the way to the Island of the Sunset Glow, using his lion-skin as a sail.

On the island the watchdog Orthos soon smelled him out and sprang at him. But Heracles struck him dead with his club, then killed the herdsman too.

Geryon proved a tougher opponent. Heracles had already started for home with the cattle and was driving them along the banks of the River of Flowers, when the three-bodied giant caught up with him. Brandishing three spears and looking fiercer than Ares the war-god himself, he hurled the spears, all three at once. Being lightly clad, Heracles skipped out of the way in time, and they landed quivering in the bank. But the giant's three huge shields, each engraved with an eagle in full flight, covered him well, and Heracles found it difficult to shoot his arrows past and reach an unprotected part. After a long struggle he succeeded, and Geryon lay dead at his feet, with an arrow through each body. Then he took the herd on board the golden cup and sailed back as far as Spain, where he returned the cup to the sun-god.

But his difficulties were not yet over. On the long overland journey home he had to swim across rivers with the herd, to drive a pass through the Alps, and to contend with many robbers, for the cattle were a rare prize. Once a three-headed, fire-belching murderer named Cacus stole four of the finest bulls and four heifers while Heracles was asleep. To confuse the tracks, he grasped them by their tails and dragged them backward into his cave.

Heracles woke at dawn and missed them at once. Unable to find them, he was driving on the rest when one of the imprisoned heifers heard them lowing and started to bellow. The hollow echoing sound soon guided him to the cave. The entrance was blocked with a huge rock, and human skulls and limbs nailed above the lintels showed what happened to strangers who tried to force a way in. But Heracles removed the rock as easily as if it had been a loose brick and went inside. Belching smoke and fire, Cacus chased him out. Then Heracles grappled with him, caught him in a wrestler's grip, and hugged him to death. The stolen cattle rejoined their fellows and he drove them on over mountain, river and plain, back to Mycenae.

9

The Golden Apples

"Fetch me the golden apples from the Garden of the Hesperides, the daughters of Night," Eurystheus ordered.

"Where is this Garden?" said Heracles.

"How should I know? I have never been there. You must find out for yourself."

Heracles had already spent eight years and a month performing his labors and had had more than enough. But he could not disobey the gods. To expiate his sin, he had promised to serve Eurystheus for twelve years.

Off he went to the west, asking everyone he met if they knew where the Garden was. In Italy some river-nymphs said that Nereus, the Old Man of the Sea, knew the answer, and they told Heracles where to find him.

"Do not go near him while he is awake," they warned.

"Seize him while he's fast asleep and cling on tight. Of course he will try to wriggle away—and he can change himself into any shape he likes. But if you cling on long enough, in the end he will return to his own shape and tell you what you want to know."

Heracles found him in a landlocked bay, an old man with a long flowing beard, fast asleep on a rock, with his fifty daughters splashing in the water. These lovely sea-nymphs lived in caves and grottoes adorned with shells and shaded with vine leaves. They had names like Eudora (Bringer of gifts), Glauke (Sea-green one), Kymodoke (Wave-gatherer), and Speio (Dweller in caves). Their hair was like seaweed tresses of gold and emerald green, and their eyes sparkled like rock pools in the sun. They liked to spend their time riding dolphins, swimming and diving, or skimming along the crests of white foam.

As soon as they saw a man coming toward them, with shrieks of delight they dropped their games and ran toward him along the sands. They crowded around him, begging him to join them. But remembering his errand Heracles declined politely, and they did not stop him when he went to their sleeping father and grasped him firmly in his arms.

Nereus woke with a shout. As Heracles tightened his grip, the bearded face became a serpent's hissing tongue. When the coils failed to crush him, the serpent changed into a leopard that tried to claw his chest, then into a lion, then a sliding river that nearly washed him out to sea. But when Nereus saw that Heracles had no intention of letting go, he became a man again and told him where the Garden was.

"It lies beyond the Ocean stream, on the edge of the world. In the middle stands the immortal tree that Mother Earth gave to Hera as a wedding present. The branches, leaves and fruit are all of shining gold. There is a high wall around the Garden to keep out thieves, and Ladon the sleepless serpent-dragon is coiled around the tree and keeps watch by night and day. Do not try to force your way in. Ask the giant Atlas to help you. He is the father of the three Hesperides, the daughters of Night, who live in the Garden, and as a punishment he carries the weight of the starry sky on his shoulders."

Heracles thanked Nereus for his help and said good-bye to his fifty daughters, who were reluctant to see him leave so soon. He journeyed on—through the land of the Scythians, who lived on cheese made from mares' milk, across the mountains of the north wind, where turbulent gusts nearly whirled him into the air—till at last he came to the Garden at the edge of the world. It was sunset, and the Ocean stream, where the horses of the sun-god were bathing their tired limbs after their long day's journey, glittered like liquid bronze. From beyond the Garden wall he heard the soft notes of the flute. Outside the wall the giant Atlas, bowed under his burden, towered above him.

"Noble Atlas, I have come to ask your help. I am Heracles, son of Zeus, and my taskmaster Eurystheus has sent me here to fetch the golden apples."

"I have been expecting you," said Atlas. "Long ago it was prophesied that a son of Zeus would come here to strip the tree."

"It belongs to Hera and is sacred to her. I dare not touch it myself."

"So you want me to do your stealing for you?" grunted Atlas. "How can I, with this great load on my shoulders?"

"I could hold it for you while you go."

Now Atlas would have done anything to ease himself for an hour or two of his appalling burden. But he hesitated.

"That serpent-dragon in the Garden never closes its eyes," he said. "I could never get past it."

"Then I will go and kill it," said Heracles, and before the giant could make any more excuses he was off.

He climbed up the wall and peered over the top into the Garden. He could not see the three daughters of Night, for they were lost among the shadows, but he could hear them playing the flute and singing. The tree of golden apples was aglow in the sunset, and the unsleeping serpent-dragon, with its long coils of twinkling scales, curled around the trunk. Quickly he fitted an arrow to his bow and shot it through the neck. With a screaming hiss it died.

He ran back to tell Atlas what he had done.

Laboriously the giant knelt on one knee, then eased his mighty sky-burden, with its countless stars and planets, onto the shoulders of Heracles. What a relief to be rid of it! He stretched himself, took several paces, and with creaking joints stepped over the wall.

Darkness was already falling as Heracles, groaning under the weight, braced himself to his terrific task. How his arms sweated, how his shoulders ached! To the ants and beetles and glowworms on the ground he seemed to be wearing a crown of stars. Slowly, very slowly the hours crept on till dawn. Then in the gray first light he saw the giant's feet striding toward him.

"I have the golden apples. Three of them," he said. "But I would like to take them to Eurystheus myself."

Now Nereus had already warned Heracles that once the giant had shed his burden he might not be in any hurry to have it back again, so he was well prepared. "Enjoy your holiday," he said, pretending to agree.

"I shall only be gone a month or two. I promise to come back. You cannot imagine how delightful it is to be free of such a load for a while."

"Well, it has not broken my back yet," said Heracles, "though I must admit it does make my head and neck rather sore. But I have a sheepskin pad, a sort of cushion, with me. If you would be kind enough to hold the sky for me for a moment, I will put the pad on my head."

"With pleasure," said the slow-witted giant. He laid the apples on the ground and resumed his load.

"Thank you," said Heracles, and he stood back to admire. "How expertly you hold the heavens in place! However long I tried, I could never hope to match your skill."

He picked up the apples and started on the long journey home.

10

The Giant and the Pygmies

Heracles did not go directly back to Mycenae, but passed through Libya first. The King of this country was Antaeus, the giant son of the sea-god Poseidon and Mother Earth. He lived in a cave under a cliff, slept on the ground, and dined off the flesh of lions. His habit was to force all the passing strangers to wrestle with him. When they were exhausted he killed them, then used their skulls to decorate his father's temple.

As soon as he saw Heracles approaching, Antaeus came thumping out of the cave, rippling his great muscles, and in a deep voice challenging him to fight.

Heracles needed no encouragement to accept the challenge. He knew all about the King's alarming habits and was determined to end them once and for all. Both prepared themselves—Antaeus by pouring sand over his limbs, and Heracles by throwing off his lion-skin and, like an Olympic athlete, rubbing himself all over with oil. Then they grappled together, writhing and twisting to and fro along the shore.

Soon Heracles was having it all his own way, for he was the stronger wrestler. But he could not reach his lofty opponent's throat. At last he forced him to his knees, then plunged his thumbs deep into either side of the giant's neck till he was limp and lifeless. Then he picked him up and, as if he were tossing his club, hurled him into the air. With a thud Antaeus landed on a rock. But to the hero's amazement, instead of breaking his back, he sprang up refreshed and threw himself back into the fight. Contact with the rock seemed to have knocked the tiredness out of him.

As they wrestled together, their limbs slippery with sweat, all the time Heracles was urging his opponent up the cliff path. At the top he caught the giant's ankle from behind with his heel and threw him off balance, then rolled him down the slope with gathering speed, like a mighty boulder. At the bottom of the cliff the giant landed with a crack that would have killed anybody else. But after he had lain there for a moment or two, hugging the sandy shore with his arms and legs, Antaeus leaped up again, with all his strength renewed.

"Ah, I understand!" cried Heracles, as the truth slowly

dawned. "You are the son of Earth. Your mother's touch puts new strength in you. You feel the earth and your muscles swell. The sand sticks to your sweating limbs and gives you power. But I shall defeat you yet."

Once more they grappled. This time Heracles caught him up and heaved him high above his head and held him there, squirming and yelling hoarsely, till all the strength drained out of the giant, as the life goes out of a fish when you keep it from the sea. Then slowly he lowered him, careful to see that no part of him, no elbow, toe or finger touched the ground. With a suffocating hug he cracked his ribs; he squeezed the breath from his lungs till he was dead. Then he hauled the corpse away and, exhausted, lay down to sleep.

And while he slept, Antaeus's brothers came. Mercifully they were not giants like himself, but pygmies, tiny dwarfs no bigger than his thumb. Eager to avenge their mighty brother's death, they prepared to attack the sleeping hero with their tiny engines of war, as if he had been a fortress. But as they crawled over him, the tickling of their feet woke him up. When he saw them, he roared with laughter.

"I must take you back to show Eurystheus," he said. "No doubt you'll frighten him out of his wits." And he picked up a handful and tucked them into his lion-skin.

Continuing his journey, Heracles went on to the Caucasus. Here he climbed the mountain to the highest crag of all, where, in the thunder and the lightning and among the roaring winds, the Titan Prometheus had stood in eternal chains for a thousand years. In the beginning of the world, when men were weak and ignorant, the noble Titan had taken pity on them and taught them how to live sensible and useful lives. But because he climbed the heavens and stole fire from the chariot of the sun, then brought it down to earth hidden in a hollow fennel stalk, Zeus was angry with him. Jealous of his power and grudging the gifts that Prometheus had brought to men, Zeus had punished him by having him fettered to the mountainside. Each day an eagle came to peck at his liver, which never grew smaller, though continually devoured. And now at long last Heracles had arrived to release him. He shot down the eagles with his arrows and set the proud unconquered Titan free.

After weeks and months of wandering he returned to Mycenae, where he was told to show his prizes.

"Here they are," said Heracles. And he took the pygmies from his lion-skin and held them out under the nose of Eurystheus. "Ferocious two-legged monsters. I captured them unaided. Do they not strike terror in your royal heart?"

Eurystheus cringed; he dared not touch them. But he gave a nervous laugh and told Heracles to put them down on the floor. Then he called his dogs to chase the pygmies around the palace for his amusement. And when he tired of the joke, he asked for the golden apples.

Heracles gave them to him. But to his surprise Eurystheus handed them back at once. This was not through any generosity on the King's part, but because he knew they belonged to Hera, and the coward was afraid that she might punish him. He would rather Heracles took all the blame.

Wisely Heracles did not keep the stolen fruit. He returned it at once to the gods.

11

An Unexpected Meeting

Heracles's final labor was the strangest of all. He was sent to the Underworld, the sacred kingdom of the dead, to capture the watchdog Cerberus, three-headed hound of Hell. One of the entrances was in Sparta through the cave of Tainaron. When he had cleansed and purified himself, he took his sword and hacked his way through the creeper-choked entrance into the gloomy tunnel. Hermes, the messenger of the gods, went with him. It was one of Hermes' duties to lead the souls of the dead on their last journey. On and on through the darkness he guided Heracles with his golden rod.

At last they reached the swampy River Styx, whose sluggish waters border the sacred kingdom. Charon, the old ferryman of the dead, was waiting to row them across.

"Have you brought me money to pay your passage, Heracles?" he shouted.

"No," said Heracles.

"Then I cannot take you across. The dead keep a coin under their tongues to pay me with."

"I am not dead—do I look it?" said Heracles. "But I can pay you if you insist—with a scowl." And he gave him such a scowl that Charon dared not refuse again.

The boat was flimsy, sewn together from pieces of bark, and Heracles came near to sinking it with his weight. But fortunately they reached the other side without shipping too much water.

Beyond them stretched a gray twilit world, without horizon. The rushy bank was crowded with ghosts, squeeking and gibbering like bats. As Heracles stepped ashore, they ran away—all but two, which stayed hovering in front of him. One was the Gorgon Medusa. He drew his sword to strike off her head before it could turn him to stone. But Hermes caught his arm and laughingly reminded him that she was only a ghost and had lost the power to do him any harm.

The other ghost was clad in shining armor and came striding toward Heracles. It was the warrior Meleager. Afraid that Hera had sent the warrior to attack him, Heracles quickly fitted an arrow to his bow.

"Do you think ghosts are as easy to kill as men?" said Meleager. "A hopeless task, even for you, Heracles. I come to you as a friend, to ask a favor. It is hardly a month since

I died. I left my sister Deianeira in my father's house, young and beautiful, and still unwed. There was no time for me to find her a husband. I know, you have no wife yourself. She would make you a good one, if you would take her."

"You feel I deserve such a prize? I will marry her gladly," said Heracles, with his usual impulsive generosity, and little realizing how fateful the consequences were to be. "But I have a pressing job to do before I can give my mind to love. I am here to fetch Cerberus. They tell me he has three heads, three manes of hissing snakes, a barbed tail—and that he likes his meat raw. But I will see he does not try his teeth on me. Where shall I find him?"

"You must cross the desolate waste to the other gate of Hades, near the River Acheron. He is chained to a stake and guards the mouth of the cave which leads up to the Caucasus and the Black Sea. But you had better ask King Hades first if you may take him."

So Heracles said good-bye to Hermes and Meleager and went off to find King Hades. First he had to cross the Elysian fields, where the spirits of the dead lived in happiness. There were flowers everywhere, motionless, with not a breath of wind to stir them; the only time they moved was when the smiling ghosts brushed past. Then he crossed a river of burning fire and came to a very different place —the smoky plain where the damned endured eternal torment for their crimes. Among them he saw Tantalus, tortured by hunger and thirst, unable to reach the fruit that dangled above him or the water that flowed past his lips;

Ixion, chained to a whirling wheel of flame; Sisyphus, forever pushing his rock uphill—down it rolled, each time it reached the top; and the daughters of Danaus, who had killed their husbands and were compelled forever to pour water into a vessel full of holes. His heart went out to all of them in their suffering.

But the sight that moved him most was something he had never expected. Above the plain of torment, on the edge of the garden of King Hades, which looked right over the kingdom, were two rocks. On each of them a man was sitting. As Heracles went by, one of them reached out his hands to him and called out his name.

It was Theseus, King of Athens, his oldest friend.

12

The Hound of Hell

Heracles had never forgotten the debt of gratitude he owed to Theseus. It was Theseus who had stood by him long ago, when Hera sent the madness and made him kill his wife Megara and his three sons. He had been crushed with guilt and despair, his life in ruins. Then Theseus had come to share his suffering and give him back his self-respect. But what was he doing here in this dismal place?

"I came here on a foolish venture, to help my friend Pirithous," said Theseus. And he pointed to the man sitting on the neighboring rock and looking even more miserable than himself. "He demanded Persephone, Queen of the Underworld, as his bride, and held me to my oath to accompany him here. It was ill-judged."

"Ill-judged indeed, and most unlike you, Theseus. But you were always one to stand by a friend, at whatever cost to yourself. But if you do not like it here, why do you stay? Get up and come with me."

"I cannot move. I am fixed to this rock, which is part of my flesh. King Hades needs no chains to keep me prisoner."

"Then I will ask him to set you free."

"He will not listen. I never harmed him or his wife, but he hates me because I came here with Pirithous. He sends the three winged Furies to torment us. They hover above us, lowing like cattle; they breathe on us with their foul breath and beat us with brass-studded whips. No, he would never listen."

"His wife Persephone would. I knew her on earth before Hades made her his queen."

For a while they talked of the past, as old friends like to do. Then suddenly Heracles saw a black chariot, drawn by black horses, coming toward them. In it were King Hades and his queen.

Persephone recognized Heracles at once. She leaped down from the chariot and greeted him affectionately, then asked him why he had come to the Underworld. So concerned was he with his friend's troubles that he almost answered, "To set Theseus free," but just in time he remembered Cerberus and his true mission.

"The hound is yours, Heracles, if you can master him," said King Hades, who was still sitting in his chariot. "But you must promise to use no weapon—no club, no sword, no arrows."

Heracles promised, then turned quickly to Persephone and tried to speak of what was uppermost in his mind. It was not easy to find excuses for an attempt at wife-stealing, especially when he was addressing the wife concerned, and even though Theseus had done nothing worse than come with Pirithous. He got so tied up with trying to express himself tactfully that Persephone laughed and readily agreed to forgive Theseus his folly.

"May he return to the world of men?" said Heracles.

"I will ask my lord," said Persephone.

"Theseus is fixed to his rock forever, and not even your strength, Heracles, can move him," said King Hades. But he added, "You may try to release him if you wish."

"Turn your eyes away, Persephone," said Heracles. "You may not like what you see."

He put down his club. Then he took hold of his friend's hands, placed his right foot against the rock and tugged with all his might. Three times he tugged, and at the third time wrenched him free. Stiff-limbed and wincing with pain, Theseus stood up. But he had left some of his skin behind —the price of his freedom, as Heracles jokingly called it.

But when with impetuous kindness he tried to release Pirithous as well, King Hades protested, and to show his displeasure he sent an earthquake that shook his whole kingdom. So it was that Theseus was allowed to go free, but Pirithous stayed behind to suffer torment forever.

At once Heracles and his old friend set off to find Cerberus. In the Elysian fields they paused to rest awhile, for Theseus was stiff and breathless. Here he made a wreath of black poplar leaves for Heracles and put it around his brows. Then they resumed their journey.

They found the watchdog at the far fringe of the Underworld, guarding the tunnel mouth and chained to a stake, as they had been told. Had they been spirits, he would have wagged his tail in greeting. But strangers made him suspicious. He gave three yelps—each had a kind of metallic ring, like the clash of a hammer on the anvil—and charged. The chain pulled him up short; the stake shuddered in the ground. Twice more he charged. The second time, Heracles sprang at him, wrapping his arms around the beast's threefold snaky neck. Squeezing hard, dodging the hissing snakes and poisonous fangs, he choked the hound till he yielded, slumped to the ground and lay motionless.

As Theseus looked at his friend, who was exhausted after his exertions, he saw that a strange thing had happened to the poplar wreath. The outer leaves were still black, but the inner leaves were bleached white by his sweat. Since that day the white poplar, whose leaves are white underneath when the wind turns them up, has been sacred to Heracles.

"I have not killed the brute, but I have broken his spirit," said Heracles. "He will know who is master when he wakes."

But when Cerberus recovered, he struggled to break free, and Heracles had to use the chain as a lead.

"Take my club, Theseus, and if he disobeys, strike him on the snout—on all three snouts."

While Heracles half-dragged, half-carried the hound, Theseus led the way into the mouth of the tunnel. It was even darker than the tunnel by which Heracles had come in. But they were able to move quickly, for the eyes of Cerberus sparkled with blue lights and were as useful as a torch.

At last they came to the cavern mouth, by the shore of the Black Sea, with the lofty Caucasus towering above.

"It seems a hundred years since I came in this way," said Theseus. "The sunlight in my eyes is like a javelin. Yet on my arms it feels warm and welcoming."

"Here by the cavern mouth the rocks and overhanging branches are white with frost," said Heracles. "I never thought that King Hades' icy breath could reach so far. It clings like a mist. Ugh!" And he strode out to meet the sun.

But Cerberus hung back, yelping with pain. He had never seen the sun before, and the white glare was blinding.

"He can see no better than a bat," said Heracles. "He'll give us little trouble now. Are you coming, Theseus?"

"No, I cannot. The torture I endured in Hades has weakened me. I must lie in the sun and sleep, until my strength returns. Go on and take the hound with you. Eurystheus will be impatient for his prize."

So Heracles took back his club from his friend and said good-bye. With Cerberus lurching at the chain—the snakes in his three manes hissing, his three mouths yelping, and a poisonous plant springing up wherever his saliva fell—the hero set off for Mycenae.

Some weeks later three children at the crossroads north of Mycenae ran screaming to the palace. They said they had just seen a three-headed monster with a dragon's spiky tail and a hundred snaky tongues hissing from its hair. As they ran in through the palace gate, Eurystheus was in the courtyard offering up a sacrifice. He just had time to reach the jar when the hound's voracious teeth caught up with him, tearing his cloak before the lid was down.

"Come out of your hole, you trembling fox!" cried Heracles, above the din of barking. "I have crossed the world for you, and the Underworld as well, and I'm as hungry as a lion!"

"I will order a banquet at once," said Eurystheus.

He was as good as his word. But he kept the best cuts for himself (served to him in his jar), and the next best for his kinsmen. To show his contempt for Heracles, he allowed him only a slave's portion.

But Heracles got the better of him in the end. By pretending to have chained Cerberus to a pillar, he at last enticed the King from his hiding place. Then he let the hound go. With three jaws snapping at his heels, Eurystheus fled in terror over the stony hills and was never seen in Mycenae again. Heracles took Cerberus back to Hades, and the hound never returned to the world of men.

So the last of the twelve labors, the most arduous and difficult tasks ever known, was accomplished.

13

The Wrestling Match

Deianeira, whom Heracles had promised the ghost of Meleager that he would marry, was the beautiful daughter of Oineus, King of Calydon. But when he came to the palace to ask her father for her hand, he found another suitor also there. This was the bearded and much respected river-god Achelous, whose silver stream flowed through Oineus's kingdom. In support of his claim Heracles reminded the King that he was the son of Zeus, a hero, and that all the world was talking of his triumphs.

"The son of Zeus?" scoffed Achelous. "I don't believe it. You are a stranger, an impostor. I am the father of Greek waters and a god, and mortals must give way to gods. . . . The son of Zeus, indeed! Doesn't everyone know that Queen Hera hates you and has driven you mad?"

Heracles glowered at him, trying hard to keep his temper. "I am no word-spinner like you," he said. "I am better at fighting than talking." And he sprang at Achelous.

After such boastful language Achelous could hardly draw back now. He threw off his green coat and put up his fists. Quickly Heracles rubbed some sand over his body, scattering a handful over the river-god as well, to make him less slippery. He caught at the river-god's neck, then his arms, then his legs. But Achelous stood as firm as a cliff battered in vain by angry seas. After awhile they drew apart, then rushed together again, each determined not to give in. Foot was entwined with foot, fingers clenched with fingers, forehead pressed against forehead. Deianeira, standing on the hillside above the river, hid her head in terror, yet all the time she hoped that Heracles would win.

Three times he tried to push the river-god away. At last he broke the hold, knocked him sideways, jumped onto his back and clung on with all his weight. Panting for breath, his arms streaming with sweat, the river-god fought to break the grip. But Heracles did not let go; he forced him to his knees.

Knowing that he could never win by strength alone, Achelous tried magic. He turned into a speckled snake and slithered out of his opponent's grasp. Then he wound his body into writhing coils, darted out his forked tongue and hissed.

But Heracles only laughed. "I used to strangle snakes when I was in my cradle," he said. "And after that I killed

the Hydra, the murderous water-snake of Lerna. He had nine heads, and you have only one. What chance have you got? You're not even a real snake." And he closed his huge hands around the river-god's neck and squeezed with all his might.

Achelous turned into a bull and charged. But Heracles, nimbly side-stepping, flung his arms around his neck and dragged him down, forcing the tips of his horns into the ground and overthrowing him. Then he tore off one of the horns.

Shamed and humiliated, Achelous retired to his river and covered the injured place with reeds and willow leaves. Some nymphs picked up the broken horn and filled it with fruit and flowers, then gave it to the joyful goddess of Abundance.

So it came about that Heracles won Deianeira and married her.

On his way home with her he came to the River Evenus, which he had to cross. To his dismay he found it swollen with winter rains, swirling with currents, and quite impassable. He might have swum across alone, but he was afraid for his young bride. While he stood hesitating on the bank, the Centaur Nessus galloped up and offered to carry her across for him. "I am the ferryman here," he said. "I know the fords and currents well and will not let her drown."

Pale and trembling, Deianeira clung to her husband. Her eyes implored him not to let her go. But the trustful Heracles laughed aside her fears and lifted her onto the Centaur's back. Waving cheerfully, he watched them splash into the water. "My club and bow will race you there," he shouted, as he threw them to the far bank. Then, still wearing his lion-skin and with his quiver strapped to his side, he dived into the roughest part and fought his way across.

As he scrambled out and was picking up his bow, he heard his wife cry out for help. The Centaur was galloping away with her.

"Thief and traitor," shouted Heracles, "how dare you steal what is not yours! Your four legs may run faster than my two, but you cannot race my arrows." And he shot one at him.

Though the Centaur was already half a mile away, it pierced him through the back, and the point stuck out of his chest. As he fell, shot to the heart, Nessus wrenched the arrow from the wound. Out spurted a stream of blood, and mixed with it the deadly poison of the Hydra, the murderous watersnake of Lerna.

"I shall have my vengeance in the end," the dying Centaur muttered. Then he turned to Deianeira and said, "Before I die, I would like to do you a favor. The blood from my wound is a powerful charm. Collect some of it, and if ever your husband's love for you grows cool, secretly anoint his shirt or cloak with it. Then his love will revive; he will never fall in love with any other woman."

Like most Greek travelers, Deianeira was carrying with her a small bottle of drinking water. Emptying it, she filled it at once with the Centaur's blood, but said nothing to Heracles. Ever afterward she kept it in her house safely hidden away.

14

The Weeping Prisoner

Heracles and Deianeira made their home at Tiryns, where a son named Hyllus and other children were born to them. Later they moved to Trachis on the Malian Gulf, not far from Mount Oeta. Although his twelve great labors were finished, Heracles could never settle down for long, and other adventures were always taking him away from home.

His last expedition was against the King of Oechalia, Eurytus, whose daughter Iole he claimed to have won in a shooting match. But when the King refused to let her go, Heracles led an army against him, killed him and his sons, and made Iole his prisoner. She refused to go back with her captor and tried to kill herself by jumping off the city wall. But the wind billowed out her bell-shaped skirt and she landed unhurt. He decided to send her in his herald's charge to his wife at Trachis, with other captive women from the city. Before returning home himself, he would stop on the Euboean headland of Cynaeum, to offer sacrifice to his father Zeus.

Meanwhile Deianeira, sad and lonely, waited for her husband's return. He had been away a whole year, and she had no idea where he was.

"Hyllus, my son, I cannot sleep at night for worrying," she said. "Before your father went away, he was warned that he might never return. The oracle at Dodona told him that after fifteen months he would either die or live in peace for the rest of his days. Can you imagine that he would ever be content with a peaceful life? He is the greatest man in the world, and I am afraid I am going to lose him."

At that moment a messenger, with a garland on his head, arrived. "My lady, your husband is safe," he told Deianeira. "He is on his way home in triumph, bringing with him the spoils of victory."

"Who told you?"

"Lichas the herald. He is down in the marketplace, with all Trachis gathered round him to hear the good news. I wanted to be the first to tell you, to earn your thanks—and perhaps some reward as well."

When Lichas and the captive women reached the palace, Deianeira and her maids were singing and dancing with joy.

"Is my husband safe? Is he alive and well?" cried Deianeira, breaking away from her companions.

"He was alive and well when last I saw him," said Lichas.

"Where was that?"

"On the headland of Cynaeum above the Euboean Sea. He was going to sacrifice to Zeus in thanks for his victory." And he told her of the quarrel with King Eurytus, how it had ended and how Heracles himself would return as soon as his thank-offerings had been made.

"Who are these women you have brought with you?"

"Your husband took them prisoner when the city fell."

"They look wretchedly unhappy. I hope no child of mine will ever suffer like this."

Her heart went out to them in pity, and to one of them in particular, a young girl who was weeping uncontrollably.

"Whose daughter are you?" asked Deianeira gently. "You look too young to be married. . . . Who is she, Lichas?"

"How should I know, my lady? But she does not look like a slave girl."

"Could she be Eurytus's child?"

"I have no idea," said Lichas, uneasily. "She weeps all the time, and no one can get a word out of her."

"We must not torment her. She has sorrows enough to bear without our adding to them. Take her into the house."

When Lichas and the young girl had gone in, the messenger took Deianeira aside and told her that the weeping captive was indeed Iole, daughter of King Eurytus, and that Heracles was madly in love with her. "I heard the herald say so in the marketplace. It was for her that he fought

Eurytus. He said she was already your husband's bride."

Obviously rumor had been busy, and rumor exaggerates everything. But Deianeira believed that what she had been told was true. Deeply shocked, she sent for Lichas.

"By the fires of God, tell me the truth about this girl," she cried. "Do you think I do not realize that a man's affections may change? Heracles has in his time loved many women. I have never blamed him or them, for I am resigned to his ways. As for this woman I was asking you about, I feel only pity for her. She cannot have wished to bring her family and country to disaster. You must not be afraid to tell me the truth about her."

Moved by Deianeira's tolerance and compassion, Lichas now confessed that the woman was indeed Iole, but that he had not wished to distress her by telling her this. "Honored lady, it would be best for you to do as your husband asks. Welcome her, do not turn her away. Send him a gift in return."

"Is there anything you know that he would specially like?"

"Yes, a ceremonial robe to wear at the sacrifice. He asked me to tell you this."

"I will do as you advise," said Deianeira, as a sudden thought sprang into her mind.

She went to her room and took from the cupboard a ceremonial robe she had just finished making for her huband. Then she fetched from the bronze jar, where she had hidden it years ago, the little water-bottle with the Centaur's

blood. Had not Nessus told her as he lay dying that, if ever her husband's love cooled, a touch of his blood would revive it and bind his heart to her again? She was growing old now, but her love for him was as fresh as it had ever been. Though she still felt pity for Iole, the thought of sharing her home with this foreign girl was more than she could bear. Smearing a tuft of wool with the Centaur's blood, she rubbed it over the lining of the robe, which she folded and took out to Lichas.

"I made it for him with my own hands," she told him proudly. "Give it to him with my love, to wear at the altar of Zeus. But he must not leave it out in the sun, and no one but he must touch it or put it on. . . . And remember too to tell him how I welcomed Iole."

As soon as Lichas had gone, Deianeira went back into the house, praying with all her heart that the charm would work. Then she picked up the tuft of wool from the floor where she had thrown it—the blood was already dry—and threw it out of the window into the courtyard. Suddenly, in the scorching sun she saw it curl up, catch fire like sawdust, then shrivel into nothing. In the place where it had been, bubbles of foam like the juice of fermenting grapes, were oozing from between the paving stones.

Her heart was filled with mortal fear. "O, what have I done?" she cried, as she realized that Nessus had tricked her. She ran from the house, calling out to Lichas to come back.

But his chariot was already over the hill, and behind the racing wheels the dust was settling.

15

The Death of Heracles

At once Deianeira sent a messenger after Lichas. By the time he reached the lonely headland of Cynaeum, Heracles was already wearing the ceremonial robe, though the poison had not yet begun to take effect. There he stood against the sky, ready to sacrifice twelve oxen at the altar. His wife's message and the splendid garment had delighted him. He looked contented and serene.

The messenger was within a spear's throw of him when Heracles, loudly thanking Zeus for his victory, began to pour wine on the flames. The heat melted the Hydra's poison, which spread through his limbs like fire. The robe clung tightly; sweat broke out on his skin, and he cried out in agony. The cliffs and rocky shore echoed with his piercing screams. When the pain was more than he could bear, he kicked over the altar and, stretching out his hands to heaven, cried out, "Look at me, cruel Hera! Feast your savage heart on my destruction. Have you no pity, even you? I beg you to let me die."

Maddened with pain, roaring like a bull with a spear through its neck, he raged along the cliff-top. He tried to tear off his robe, to root up bushes and trees.

Suddenly he saw Lichas cowering in a rocky hollow, clasping his knees in terror.

"Was it you, Lichas, that brought this fatal gift?" he shouted. "Did you plot to kill me?"

The herald trembled and turned pale. He made excuses. "I know of no plot. The gift was from your wife, and I brought it in all innocence, I swear."

Heracles seized him by an ankle, swung him three times above his head, then hurled him—swift as a bolt from a catapult—far out to sea. The herald's body stiffened in mid-air; his blood froze, like rain turned to ice in the bitter wind. As he splashed into the Euboean Sea, he turned into a rock. This rock in human shape can still be seen today, but sailors are terrified to go near it.

Wrapped in swirling smoke, Heracles sped on, till at last he fell exhausted to the ground. In the crowd of faces around him he caught a glimpse of his son Hyllus, who had followed hard on the messenger's heels to seek out his father.

"Hyllus, do not hide from me," he said. "I do not want

to die here. Take me quickly somewhere else, where I can die in peace."

Gently Hyllus lifted him onto a stretcher and with a companion carried him down to the shore, where a boat was waiting. They laid him in the hold, groaning and crying out that his wife had sent the poisoned robe to kill him. As they rowed him to the mainland, the motion of the boat and the lapping water rocked him into a fitful sleep, from which the grinding of the keel on the far shore momentarily woke him. They laid his stretcher on the sand, at the edge of the pinewoods, and he slept again, then woke to find friends about him and Hyllus bending over him with tears in his eyes.

"While you were asleep, father, a messenger came from Trachis with the saddest news. Deianeira is dead."

"Dead, you say? Who dared to kill her? How did she die?"

"In anguish and remorse she stabbed herself on her marriage bed."

"I ought to have killed her myself."

"You would not say that if you knew the truth. She loved you, she wanted to win you back."

"By trying to kill me? It was a strange way to choose."

"She never meant to hurt you," said Hyllus. And he explained what his mother had told him before she died—about the love-charm and how the Centaur had deceived her.

There was a silence. Then, with a hopeless sigh, Heracles said, "Now I understand. . . . There was once a prophecy that no living man could kill me, only a dead enemy. It is now fulfilled."

Breathing in the sweet scent of the pinewoods, he gazed beyond them to the summit far above. It was Mount Oeta, sacred to Zeus, and he recognized it.

"Carry me to the topmost peak and build me a funeral pyre of oak and wild olive. Lay me on it—no tears, no grief, mind you—then take a pine-torch and set fire to it."

"Father, you are asking too much," said Hyllus, appalled. "How can I consent to be your murderer?"

"Not my murderer. My doctor and savior," said Heracles. "Death is the only cure for my sickness, and I must go and find him, as he is slow to come to me. One other thing I ask. You know about Iole, the daughter of Eurytus? As soon as you are of age, I want you to marry her."

The prospect of marrying the woman who had been the cause of his mother's death was displeasing to Hyllus. But he knew that to defy his father in his hour of death would be a greater sin. With deep reluctance, he agreed.

Tenderly they carried the stretcher to the topmost peak of Mount Oeta, as Heracles had asked. They cut down trees and built a funeral pyre; they laid him on it and lit the pine-torch. But at the last moment Hyllus flinched from his dreadful task—he could not bear to destroy his father. A youth named Philoctetes took the torch from his trembling hand and set the pyre alight, while Heracles gratefully gave the youth his bow and quiverful of arrows. Then, as the

greedy flames licked around him, he lay back on his lion-skin. With his club for pillow and a happy smile on his face, he did not look like a man about to die, but like a guest at banquet, crowned and garlanded, reclining on his couch among the cups of wine.

The flames crackled fiercely as they devoured the withered flesh. Yet he showed no sign of fear and did not wince or cry. From high Olympus the gods looked down; and Father Zeus, well pleased, gave him his blessing and said, "My favorite son has triumphed and overcome. He will overcome these flames as well, for part of him is immortal and he will not die. I will make him a god, for he deserves to be one, whatever you gods and goddesses may think."

This rebuke was aimed at Hera and she did not like it. But she said nothing, for even she was feeling pity at last, and the hardness in her heart began to melt. Later she came to regard Heracles as her own son, and when she knew him truly there was no one in heaven save Zeus that she loved more.

So the fire rushed up and the body of Heracles disappeared. Like a snake that has shed its old skin, he seemed to put on a new heroic body, more vigorous and majestic than before. Then Zeus sent his four-horse chariot through the clouds to fetch him. With ringing peals of thunder he welcomed him to heaven among the stars.